CW00762058

Dippy
And His First Adventure
To Earth

Olivia Collins

First published in 2004 by:
Olivia Collins

© Copyright 2004
Olivia Collins

The right of Olivia Collins to be identified as the author of this
work has been asserted by her in accordance with the Copyright,
Designs and Patents Act 1988.

All Rights Reserved
No reproduction, copy or transmission of this publication may be
made without written permission. No paragraph of this
publication may be reproduced, copied or transmitted save with
the written permission or in accordance with the provisions of the
Copyright Act 1956 (as amended).

ISBN:0-9548852-0-1

Illustrations by Hugh Howard

Printed and bound in Great Britain by:
ProPrint, Riverside Cottages, Old Great North Road, Stibbington,
Cambridgeshire PE8 6LR

Dippy
And His First Adventure
To Earth

CONTENTS

FOREWORD

Dippy is an adorable little alien, a character certain to endear himself to young children.

The story will fire the imagination of its readers and enable them to relate to Dippy and Mink's adventures and experiences.

I am sure children will benefit from the educational elements of the story and gain enjoyment from reading this amusing little book.

Louise Causon

INTRODUCTION

Dippy is the story of a little alien and his brother, Mink, who lived on the planet Dyfuss.

It tells of their first trip to Earth and the dangers they have to overcome on the way, as well as all the exciting new things they experience.

I hope you enjoy reading this, the first of Dippy's adventures.

Olivia Collins

DEDICATED to my two grandsons,
Jacob and Toby,
without whose persistent encouragement this book
might never have been completed.

NOTE:

The main characters in this book speak Dyfussian but since there are only a handful of humans who know the language, it has been translated into English to make understanding easier for the reader.

Chapter 1

Leaving Home

Dipando, Dippy to his family and friends, was a young alien. He was created on the planet Dyfuss where he lived with his parents and a pest of a slightly younger brother called Mink.

Dipando, Dippy to his family and friends, was a young alien

Dippy, although a thoroughbred Dyfussian, had hopes and dreams just like Earthlings. He longed to be able to travel to other worlds and to learn about other cultures. Above all he wanted to visit planet Earth. He'd learned a lot about it from his grandparents and facts about what Earthlings ate and the games they played had been programmed into him when he was created. It all seemed very different from the life he led on Dyfuss.

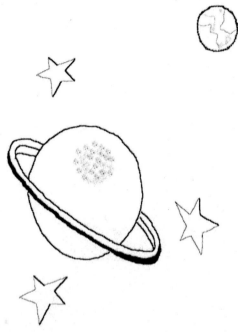

"Keep it a secret, but I am planning to go to Earth".

One day, whilst out walking in space with his brother Mink he said, "Keep it a secret, but I am planning to go to Earth."

"Don't make me laugh," scoffed Mink, "where are you going to get the tokens to get a ticket on a space shuttle?"

"Well," said Dippy indignantly, "I'm going to hide on board when no-one is looking."

"Huh, I'd like to see you do it," mocked Mink.

"Just watch me then!" retorted Dippy.

So each night for a week, Dippy watched the news on his computer, taking notes whenever the newsreader spoke about what was happening with space travel until he had all the data he needed to formulate a plan.

He had heard his parents talking about the lack of security at the Ibrax space station and how easy it would be for someone to get past the guards and onto the shuttle. Dippy was getting very excited.

That day, as Dippy and Mink were tucked up in bed (Dyfussians slept in the day and were active at night), having put their batteries on charge and cleaned their antennae and flushed out their food tubes and as their father read to them about history on planet Dyfuss for the hundredth time, Dippy's thoughts were on plans for his adventure. He had already packed a little suitcase with what he'd need – the toy Earthling his grandma had given him last Christmas, his pocket computer and some spare batteries, an old rug and their foil suits. He had also managed to sneak some chocolate pills and a bottle of red fire juice from the kitchen in case he got hungry or thirsty on the journey.

All the excitement made Dippy tired and it wasn't long before he drifted off to sleep.

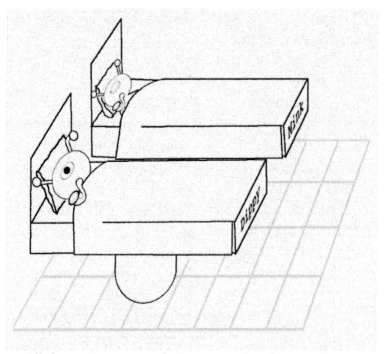

*All the excitement made Dippy tired and it wasn't long
before he drifted off to sleep.*

The Dyfuss wild dogs were howling so much
they woke Dippy up. He sat up in bed and looked at
his watch. The watch spoke quietly "The time is
twenty light years past eight." *Goodness me*, Dippy
thought to himself, *time for me to leave.* He
climbed out of bed, tiptoed across the room and
pulled out his suitcase from the back of the
cupboard. Suddenly the light came on and Dippy
turned, startled.

"Where are you going?" asked Mink, sitting up in his bed.

"Nowhere," replied Dippy as innocently as he could.

"Oh yes you are," said Mink; "you're off on your trip aren't you?"

"Might be," said Dippy pretending to be cool.

"Well, unless you take me with you, I'll scream out for Mum." (Mink wasn't a very pleasant alien brother).

"Shhh . . ." whispered Dippy, "or you will spoil my plans. You can come with me if you promise to do what I say. After all, it is my idea."

"OK," said Mink, gathering some bits together in a bag. "Let's go."

Dippy and Mink crept out of their room, past their parent's room, down a long corridor and through the main door from their home space station.

"Mind the ground beetles," warned Dippy, "they can give you a nasty bite."

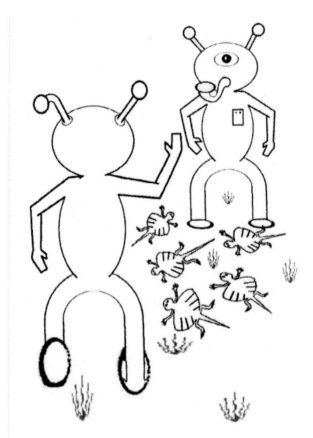

"Mind the ground beetles," warned Dippy, "they can give you a nasty bite."

Mink looked down. The ground was swarming with beetles, scurrying about. They crunched beneath his feet as he walked. The boys hurried away from their home as fast as they could, their luggage in one hand and their direction finders in the other.

"It's this way," said Dippy, referring to his notes. "I've keyed in our destinations into my direction finder and it's pointing straight ahead towards the planet Phoo."

"I'm coming, I'm coming," said Mink breathlessly, trying hard to keep up with his brother who was, apparently, fitter than he was.

They seemed to walk for ages, their luggage felt heavier and they were getting hungry.

"We can't stop yet," said Dippy in his commanding voice. "We will have a rest and a chocolate pill as soon as we reach Acad town. According to my direction finder we will be halfway to the shuttle station then."

Mink nodded reluctantly. He was already wishing he had stayed in bed but they had come too far to turn back and, in any case, he was afraid of the light. *Better to stay together*, he thought to himself.

Chapter 2

Journey Via The Frozen Forest

Light years later they reached the outskirts of Acad. They found a sponge pool, soft and springy and sat down in it to rest. Dippy fished around in his case and pulled out two chocolate pills.

"Here," he said, passing one to his brother. "This will give you some energy."

Mink grabbed the pill and popped it into his food tube. "Mmmm, that's good" he said, dribbling chocolate down the front of himself as he spoke.

"We can't stay long," ordered Dippy, "you had better recharge your battery before we go any further."

Mink nodded, took the lead from his battery pack and plugged it into Dippy's computer, watching the screen until it read 'FULL POWER' then he lay back in the sponge pool for a further moment's rest.

He must have dozed off because the next thing he knew, Dippy was shaking him and saying "Come on, it's time to go."

Mink got to his feet. He felt a bit dopey but as Dippy was in charge he did as he was asked and gathered up his bag and off they went. The ground was very rough on this part of the journey and they had to keep dodging round the hot spurts of lava, red and bubbling beneath their feet.

"Ouch!" yelped Mink, "that was hot."

"Do be careful," advised Dippy, "I didn't bring any healing oil with me."

Despite the warning, Mink ended up with blisters and burns on his feet and walking became very uncomfortable.

Later, rather than sooner, they reached the town of Acad. The place was deserted since the people of Acad, like Dyffusians, slept during the day.

Dippy and Mink kept close to the buildings, hiding in the shadows to avoid being spotted by any early risers. They passed by stores selling all manner of weird things. Mink spotted a model kit of a famous Earthling. He had always wanted one but it cost five thousand tokens and he didn't have that many.

"Mink, come on," urged Dippy, "we have to get through town before anyone wakes up and starts asking us questions."

Mink reluctantly dragged himself away from the store window and ran quickly to catch up with his brother.

"I'm tired," moaned Mink, "can't we find somewhere to sleep?"

"Soon," said Dippy sympathetically, "once we get out of Acad and into the Frozen Forest."

Mink sighed. He wished he were as strong and brave as his brother. He didn't fancy the sound of the Frozen Forest one little bit but he was too weary to argue.

"It's going to feel colder in the forest."

Dippy was on a high – excitement had got the better of him and he hadn't given a second thought to the worry they might be causing their parents. Mink on the other hand, wished with all his heart that he could be back with his Mum. He would give her such a kiss and a hug – not something he did very often.

"Do come on," urged Dippy, "or we'll never get there."

He grabbed Mink's hand and virtually dragged him along until they were clear of Acad. Ahead of them they could see the edges of the Frozen Forest.

"Best put on a cover," advised Dippy, "it's going to feel colder in the forest but it's also a good place to hide and to sleep for a while."

They consulted their direction finders and headed off towards the forest, taking a left turn across the first of many icy streams.

"Crikey, it's cold here," said Mink, who much preferred to be warm and comfortable.

"Don't be such a pathetic wimp," grunted Dippy, "no-one would believe you were almost six years old."

"Don't shout at me," said Mink, starting to cry, "this was a stupid idea anyway."

"Baby, baby," teased Dippy unkindly. "OK, OK, I didn't mean it," he said, apologetically. "We will stop here and get some sleep."

He found a small ice cave and crept inside, beckoning Mink to follow. "We'll be safe in here."

He laid out a small rug for them to lie on, set the alarm on his watch and before long they were both fast asleep.

After what must have been a number of light years later, Dippy woke up. He rubbed his eyes and looked round. For a moment he was confused – it didn't look like his bedroom. Then he remembered, he was on an adventure. He sat up. Mink was still fast asleep beside him. He prodded him, gently.

"Mink, wake up." Mink stirred, opened his eye, promptly shut it again and went back to sleep. Dippy prodded him again, this time a bit harder.

"Mink, wake up," he said.

Mink turned over onto his back. "Leave me alone, I'm tired," he moaned.

"Listen, we've got to get going again. First we will have some juice and a Wacky Wafer. I forgot I had them in my pocket."

At the mention of Wacky Wafers, Mink jumped up, grabbing one from Dippy's hand.

"Steady on," said Dippy, you nearly pulled my fingers off!"

Dippy and Mink sat quietly, eating and drinking and pondering what they should do next. They consulted the map that Dippy had drawn up and, referring to their direction finders, decided that the quickest and safest route to the shuttle station would be to skirt around the forest – going through it might hold dangers they didn't know about and they weren't that brave. That would bring them to a small village, long since deserted by a nomadic tribe of aliens called the Metrons.

After that their route would pass through the town of Bathos – they'd have to be very careful, because Dippy remembered that one of his relatives lived there.

Once through Bathos it was a straight road across the mighty Dellor Desert and the shuttle station should be visible from there.

"Simple," said Dippy, trying to hide his concern. Inwardly he was wondering now whether this adventure was such a good idea but he couldn't possibly let Mink know his fears or else he would have a babbling, whining little brother to contend with and he had enough problems already.

Fully refreshed they packed up their bits and pieces, folded up the rug on which they had been sleeping, brushed and kicked the Earth beneath them so as not to leave any clues that they had been around and set off back the way they had come till they were clear of the forest.

"Quiet," whispered Dippy, "I can hear someone coming."

They ducked down behind a huge rock, their antennae tucked down so as they wouldn't be seen.

They ducked down behind a huge rock,

They heard voices getting louder and the marching of feet.

"It must be a security patrol," said Dippy nervously. Mink shuffled over closer to Dippy, he was scared.

"Shhhh, put your head down and keep very still," said Dippy.

Mink shut his eye tight and snuggled up to Dippy for comfort. Through a crack in the rock he could just see about four big, tall guards going past.

"One two, one two, one two" they chanted. After what seemed an eternity the pounding of feet and the voices disappeared into the distance.

"Phew, that was close," said Dippy.

They gathered themselves together and cautiously crept out from behind the rock. There was no sign of the guards and so they set off in an easterly direction, around the edge of the forest until they came to a small sign, which read THIS WAY TO METRONIA.

"That's where we want to go," said Dippy, pointing to the sign. It's not far. We will have a scout round when we get there just in case the Metrons have left anything of use to us. I think we could do with some more supplies."

Chapter 3

To Metronia And Bathos

The boys walked and walked, chatting amiably about the things that interest young aliens – computers, food, computers, drink, computers, toys and so on. Soon they reached the village of Metronia. It was very, very quiet. Not a scuffle or a whistle or anything.

"I don't like it here" said Mink nervously, "it's scary."

"I know," said Dippy. "I've never been anywhere so quiet. Let's investigate."

Mink kept very close to Dippy, in fact by accident he tripped him up.

"Ouch!" shouted Dippy, "look where you are going!"

He picked himself up off the ground, rubbing his antennae, which had got a bit bent in the fall.

"Sorry," said Mink, "I didn't do it on purpose."

The pair passed what looked to be an old supplies store.

"Let's go in here," said Dippy, "there might be something worth having."

They pushed their way through the old rickety door. It creaked as they opened it and Mink grabbed Dippy in fright.

"Get off me, you lemon!" said Dippy crossly.

They looked round. As luck would have it the place didn't seem to have been ransacked as they had expected. They found some packets of biscuits, not their favourite but they couldn't afford to be fussy. Dippy found a can of some drink or other. He couldn't read the label because it was written in Metronian and he didn't understand it.

"Never mind, it will be better than nothing," said Dippy hoping that it wasn't anything too harmful. They found bits of rope and a knife, which they thought might be useful and stuffed all their goodies into Mink's bag.

"Oh," moaned Mink, "it's too heavy for me to carry."

"Well, I'll take the bag and you can carry my suitcase," said Dippy.

So they did a swap. Actually the suitcase was just as heavy but Mink thought he had better not say anything or else Dippy might get touchy. They left the store and went back out into the street. Despite being dark the air was heavy.

"Looks like it might rain," said Dippy.

Mink said nothing. In fact he didn't say anything for quite a while. He just walked.

As it was getting dark that meant people would be waking up, time for them to hide and grab some sleep. They found a cellar inside one of the stores and although the place smelled a bit from being empty so long, they were so tired that they could sleep anywhere. Mink spread out their rug and they were soon both fast asleep.

They awoke to a day with howling winds. It was a bit eerie to listen as the wind whistled through gaps in the walls.

"I'm scared" said Mink, his body shaking with fear.

"It's alright, come closer. You will be safe with me," said Dippy in his older-brother voice.

They consulted their map and the direction finders.

"Next stop is Bathos," said Dippy. "According to my reckoning, we should reach it within just two light years. Then it gets a bit more difficult when we have to cross the Dellor desert."

"Next stop is Bathos," said Dippy

Once more they gathered all their belongings together and before leaving, did a quick top up to their batteries. It would be disastrous if they ran out of power out in the open.

They climbed the rickety steps back up from the cellar and looked around to make sure they weren't being watched. It looked safe enough. Dippy walked towards the door but before he could step outside, he heard a horrific scream from Mink. He dropped his baggage and raced back inside, only to find Mink cowering in a corner, shaking with fright and pointing a finger down towards the ground.

Dippy looked and there was the sweetest little moonbug you've ever seen, its bright eye shining as it hid in the shadows.

"For goodness sake, Mink. Look, it's only a moonbug. He is as frightened as you are."

"For goodness sake Mink. Look, it's only a moonbug."

"Wwwww . . . ell," stammered Mink, "I saw an eye shining in the darkness and I thought it was a space spectre."

"Come on," said Dippy, "let's get going."

This time Mink stayed very close to Dippy. Dippy picked up his case from where he had hurriedly dropped it and they set off once more towards the town of Bathos.

This part of their journey was uneventful apart from passing through a swarm of blue-eared bugs. One flew right into Dippy's eye causing him to yelp in pain, but the pain soon passed.

Just as Dippy had predicted, they very soon reached the town of Bathos. He remembered too that one of his relatives lived here. He couldn't quite remember just who it was but he was taking no chances. They proceeded with extreme caution. The place was quiet, only one or two Bathpets were around, probably those working late in the crystal mines.

The crystals mined in Bathos were amongst the best and most powerful on the entire planet. Dippy and Mink had been shown one by their grandfather. It was big and it shone and twinkled. Their grandfather kept it locked up in a box of precious things, promising that when they were older, the crystal would be theirs provided that they used its power wisely.

The crystal would be theirs provided that they used it's power wisely.

Mink said, "I'm hungry. Have we got any more chocolate pills or juice left?"

"Well," said Dippy in a very superior tone, "you can have just one pill but I am saving the juice for the journey across the desert."

"OK," said Mink, "that will do me for now."

He gratefully took a chocolate pill from the packet Dippy offered him and popped it into his food tube.

"Yummy, that was good. Aren't you having one too Dippy?"

"No," replied Dippy, "we might be glad of it later."

As they journeyed on, Dippy and Mink talked about what they would do on Earth when they reached it.

"I want to try their food," said Mink, who was always concerned about keeping his food tube full.

"I want to learn about their animals," said Dippy "and I have seen on the computer back home how Earthlings like to go on dangerous rides. Mummy says they're stupid but I think it looks like fun."

"Me too," agreed Mink, who always liked to copy his brother anyway.

Before long they were clear of Bathos. Ahead of them lay the Dellor desert, probably the most dangerous part of their adventure.

Chapter 4

The Dellor Desert
And A Shortcut Through The Maze

"Let's rest here a while," suggested Dippy. "We need to plan the rest of our journey with great care."

"Why's that?" questioned Mink.

"Because for one thing we have to make our rations last and secondly we must be careful to avoid all the nasty bugs and creatures that roam the desert," replied Dippy.

"What bugs and creatures?" shouted Mink. "You didn't tell me there were bugs and things."

"Also," continued Dippy, ignoring Mink's little outburst, "we have to reach the shuttle station by the year 2960 if we are to get to Earth as planned."

Dippy sat quietly, inputting data into his computer.

"According to my reckoning" he said, "we have only a few light years in which to reach the shuttle station. We have no time to waste."

Once more the two little aliens packed up their belongings and set off. Ahead of them they could see the heat mist rising from the desert.

As they plodded on, Mink as usual lagging behind, Dippy said, "You will need to cover up before we reach the desert."

"Whatever for?" Mink asked indignantly.

"Because, my dear little brother, you will need protection from the biting bugs. They say the Lunar Locusts are huge out here, to say nothing of the stinging sandbugs."

"That's it then!" said Mink, stamping his foot in temper, "I'm not going any further!"

"Please yourself, but I'm going on and I can't see you finding your way back to Dyfuss on your own," retorted Dippy.

Mink thought for a moment or two.

"OK," he said, "I'll come but only because you will need my help."

Dippy smiled to himself but said nothing.

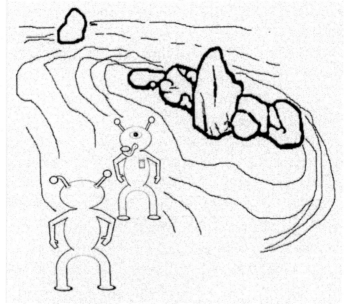

"It's jolly hot here," observed Mink.

In a matter of a few light years they had arrived at the Dellor desert. As far as they could see there was nothing but grey sand. The scene was scary. There were no plants to be seen, no buildings and no people. Just the odd sand hill and a few rocks. Mink moved closer to Dippy for protection as the pair took their first footsteps onto the grey sand.

"It's jolly hot here," observed Mink.

"I know, but you should still cover up," warned Dippy.

They paused, took out their silver foil covers and put them on. Just their faces, hands, feet and antennae remained exposed.

"See that hill over there in the distance?" pointed out Dippy. "When we reach that we will drink and eat, just a little and perhaps sleep for a short while."

Mink nodded in agreement. His food tube was bubbling with gas because it was almost empty and he could hardly keep his eye open he was so tired.

It was deathly quiet in the desert. Just the occasional buzzing swarm of Lunar Locusts broke the silence.

"How much further?" Mink whined.

"I told you," said Dippy, "when we reach that hill, we will rest."

They plodded on. It was difficult walking on the sand. Each footstep became an effort. Mink stopped for a while to watch a colony of sandbugs, which he had disturbed. When he looked up again, Dippy was way ahead of him.

"Wait for me!" he called as he tried to run to catch him up.

By the time he reached Dippy's side, he was exhausted.

"Phew, I'm tired," said Mink breathlessly.

"It's OK, we're almost at the hill now," replied Dippy.

The hill cast a big shadow and the pair settled down in its shade, glad to get out of the intense heat. Their foil suits helped too though they made a crinkly noise when they moved. Dippy dug deep into his case and took out the bottle of liquid he had found back in Metronia.

"Here, have a few sips of this," said Dippy.

Mink took the bottle gratefully and gently tipped a few drops of the blue liquid into his food tube.

"Wow! That was good. I needed that," said Mink, passing the bottle back to Dippy who also poured a small amount of the liquid into his tube.

They also had two chocolate pills each. Then they topped up their battery supplies before settling down for a rest. Whatever was in that strange, blue liquid had made them very sleepy and when Dippy eventually stirred and glanced at his watch, fear struck.

"Wake up, Mink!" he shouted. "We've been asleep for ages and I don't think we've got enough time to get to the shuttle station for our flight to Earth."

Mink opened his eye then promptly shut it again.

"Mink! Mink!" shouted Dippy crossly.

Mink didn't move until a swift, hard kick to his shins did the trick.

"Ouch! What did you do that for?" asked Mink, rubbing his now sore leg.

"Come on, we've got to get going, though I can't see how we are to get to the shuttle in time now," explained Dippy, almost in tears.

"Why don't you ask your computer for an alternative route?" suggested Mink, proud that he should come up with such a good idea.

"Brilliant!" said Dippy, keying information into the computer. After a few minutes the computer bleeped to let them know it had an answer.

"It says we can take a short-cut through a maze which will bring us out on the other side of the desert," said Dippy.

"Let's do it then," replied Mink.

"Well, it's not as simple as that. If we get lost in the maze then we will miss the flight for sure," explained Dippy.

The pair sat discussing their dilemma but came to the conclusion that they had nothing to lose by attempting to get quickly through the maze.

Dippy keyed into his direction finder then said, "According to this, the maze is just ahead of us though I can't see anything through this heat mist."

"Never mind," replied Mink, "let's go anyway. The direction finder has been right up until now."

Dippy nodded and, gathering up their belongings, they set off.

As they walked on, the heat mist seemed to clear and there lay the maze, an endless path, banked by huge rocks and sand walls, weaving in and out. The sight of the maze gave the two aliens encouragement. In fact, Mink almost ran to the entrance. Just by stood a large sign. Not a sign like on Earth, with writing on it but what looked like a large box, with a kind of opening in it.

Suddenly a voice boomed out from the box.

"Beware the maze is full of evil. Take care all who enter."

Mink turned to Dippy, his little legs shaking.

"Wwwwwww . . . e can't go in there. It's ddd . . . dangerous," he cried.

"Don't worry," said Dippy, "I'll take good care of you."

Mink grabbed Dippy's hand for comfort. *Good job my friends can't see me holding my brother's hand or they would call me names,* he thought to himself. Right now though he didn't care, he was too frightened.

Keeping close to each other, the pair stepped through the gates whilst the sign carried on calling out, *"BEWARE, TAKE CARE ALL WHO ENTER."*

"This doesn't look very scary," observed Dippy, "it's just sand and rocks."

Mink's legs were still shaking.

"I'm not so sure," he said and put out a hand onto one of the rocks to steady himself. With that the rock split in two, the upper part lifted up like a lid and a huge moon snake slithered out. It was bright red with huge bulging eyes. Both Dippy and Mink screamed in fear and ran away as fast as they could. They eventually had to stop to rest and allow their batteries to recharge. They turned round slowly just in time to see the moon snake returning into its rock.

"Wow! That was close!" said Dippy. "I hope we don't see any more of them!"

Mink was so scared he couldn't speak at all.

A huge moon snake slithered out.

The paths wound their way back and forth until they came to a flat area of sand with just a few stones along the edge.

"Can we rest now?" pleaded Mink.

Dippy nodded and said, "OK, but let's just get to the other side of this clearing."

He took two steps forward when suddenly, the ground opened up in front of him and he disappeared down into a huge, dark pit. He landed with quite a thump.

Mink peered over the edge and called out "Dippy, are you alright?"

"I'm a bit sore but I think I am still in one piece. Try and find a way to get me out of here."

Mink thought, then he remembered the bits of rope they had collected from the store in Metronia. He took them from his bag and tied lengths of rope together, put one end around his little waist and tossed the other end into the pit.

"Here, take this and I will try and pull you out," he called to Dippy.

"But you are smaller and weaker than me," replied Dippy.

"For once in your life, trust me," said Mink crossly.

Slowly and surely, somehow he managed to pull Dippy out of the pit.

"Phew! Thanks, Mink, you're a star," said Dippy gratefully as he sat resting.

Mink just glowed with pride.

Slowly and surely, somehow he managed to pull Dippy out of the pit.

After a little while the pair set off again, up and down the twisting paths until they reached what looked like a small lake.

"I didn't expect to find this in a desert," said Dippy. "How are we to get across?"

"Swim, I guess," replied Mink, wishing with all his might he'd got his water wings with him.

"Here, give me your bag and I will try and throw it across the water."

Mink passed Dippy his bag and with one huge throw, the bag landed on the other side. Dippy took his own case and did the same with that.

"Now," said Dippy, "we just have to get ourselves across."

The water looked clear and inviting. Dippy dangled his toes into the water and said, "Come on Mink, it's lovely and cool. I will help you."

Mink reluctantly dipped in one foot and then the other, just as Dippy splashed down into the water.

"Wait for me!" yelled Mink. "You know I can't swim very well."

"It's not deep," said Dippy as he gently lifted Mink down into the water beside him.

They slowly and carefully paddled their way across the lake but with just a little way left to go, they heard a mighty roar coming from behind them. They stopped to look and there, before their very eyes, rose a huge monster. It was grey, with a tail along which were fierce looking spikes. The monster thrashed its tail back and forth in the water.

"Watch out, Mink, that tail could do us great injury."

The little aliens swam as they'd never done before, even Mink forgot he had no water wings to support him.

Dippy reached safety first and grabbed Mink, pulling him out of the water after him. With a final roar the monster disappeared back down into the water.

"If I had known, I would never have come on this adventure," moaned Dippy.

"Don't worry," said Mink, shaking the water out of his antennae tops, "I can see the end of the maze just ahead and then we will be almost at the shuttle station."

With this thought in mind, the pair set off with renewed energy, determined to reach the transport, which would take them to Earth.

The pair set off with renewed energy, determined to reach the transport which would take them to Earth.

Chapter 5

At The Shuttle Station And The Journey Through Space

Dippy consulted his computer watch.

"We must hurry now, or we will miss our chance to get on the Earth shuttle."

As they neared the space station, they could see two huge rockets, each with a shuttle fixed to its side.

"How do we know which one goes to Earth?" enquired Mink.

"I'm not sure," replied Dippy, "but if you read out the big numbers painted on the rockets, I will key them into the travel pages on this computer and that will tell us."

"B3580MK" and C2560J," called out Mink.

Dippy tapped the numbers into the computer.

"That's the one!" exclaimed Dippy. "That's the one that will take us to Earth."

The two little aliens could hardly contain their excitement. Dippy couldn't believe they had even got this far. Not in his wildest dreams could he have imagined the scene now in front of him.

The two rockets were huge. So tall, neither Dippy nor Mink could see the top of them. There were lots of buildings. Vehicles were being driven to and from the rockets and there were security men everywhere, just like those that Dippy and Mink had seen outside the Frozen Forest.

The rockets were huge.

"We're going to have to be very careful now," warned Dippy. "Somehow we have to get past all those guards without being seen."

"That won't be easy," said Mink, gazing all around and noting that the guards were armed with laser guns.

They took the opportunity to take a last sip of juice and a final chocolate pill each, plugged in their batteries for a last charge and then sat quietly, planning what to do next.

After a little while Dippy whispered, "Watch that guard in the yellow suit. It takes him exactly three space minutes to reach from one end of his patrol to the other and each time he gets close to that gatehouse, he pauses to chat to the man at the barrier. I think, if we are really quick, we could run around the edge of this yard, over to that huge pile of crates. From behind them we could time it precisely so that we get under the barrier whilst the guard is talking. What do you think?"

Mink thought for a moment then said, "I haven't got a better idea so let's go for it!"

They gathered up their belongings and waited for the right moment.

"Keep really close to me," said Dippy sternly.

Mink had no intention of doing anything else. He was both scared and excited at the same time.

"Are you ready? OK, let's go NOW!"

With that, they ran as fast as their little legs would allow and literally threw themselves onto the ground behind the pile of crates.

"That was close," said Dippy. "I thought the guard with the silver helmet had seen us for sure."

"Perhaps he did," said Mink, "and perhaps he thought he must be dreaming to see two little aliens running about, one carrying a bag and the other a suitcase!"

The pair chuckled quietly to themselves.

"Now for the difficult bit," said Dippy seriously. "Look carefully Mink. Beyond the barrier there is a small building to the left."

"Which side is left?" asked Mink innocently.

Dippy sighed. "It's that one for goodness sake!" he said impatiently, pointing to the left.

"Oh," replied Mink.

"Now, when I say *go*, we have to run around the edge of this yard, get under the barrier and round the back of that building. Do you think you can do that without getting caught?"

"Gosh, I hope so," said Mink. "I don't fancy being taken prisoner that's for sure."

"Right, now pay attention. When I tap you on the arm you must run with me as fast as you possibly can, keeping right behind me."

"OK," said Mink.

Almost at once he felt a tap on his arm and he started to get up. Dippy grabbed him by the leg and pulled him back down onto the ground.

"What on earth are you doing?" he said. "I told you not to move until I tapped your arm."

"But you did, I felt it," pleaded Mink.

Dippy smiled. "You idiot, it was the strap of your bag flapping about. Good job I stopped you or you would have been caught for sure."

They sat quietly, recovering from that close call. Dippy concentrated on timing the guard's patrol.

"Ready? Let's go!"

They ran and ran, darting in and out of the shadows, under the barrier and round the back of the little building. They were so exhausted that they lay there for some time without speaking a word.

Then Dippy said, breathlessly, "Wow! We made it. We actually made it!"

He was so relieved he gave Mink a big hug.

"We can't stay here for long," said Dippy. "It's too dangerous. We need to get onto the shuttle soon. I can already see some Bathpets and some Acadians going up the steps."

"We can't go up the steps can we?" asked Mink. "We haven't got tickets."

"I know, I know," said Dippy. "We've got to get round the back of the shuttle and into the luggage hold somehow."

They sat and watched until Mink leaned over to Dippy and said, "What about us climbing into one of those huge crates they are loading into the shuttle? I think we would fit, we are only little."

Dippy smiled then said, "For a pest of a little brother you're not so bad. It's a brilliant idea."

"Glad to help," replied Mink proudly.

"There's not so far to run this time, but there are more guards so we must be extra vigilant," said Dippy.

They sat discussing their final dash until Dippy said they had to go or the opportunity would be gone. They watched as crate after crate was loaded into the hold of the shuttle.

"Look," said Dippy, "see that huge brown crate, the one without a lid? Let's go for that one."

So, in a final rush, they raced the last short distance, flinging themselves and their baggage into the brown crate, pulling boxes and all sorts over them. They lay there, bruised and battered, too scared to move. They heard voices shouting and then suddenly felt themselves being lifted up in the crate and a whirring noise as they swung through the air and then down again. They moved closer to each other for comfort and lay there silently for what seemed an eternity.

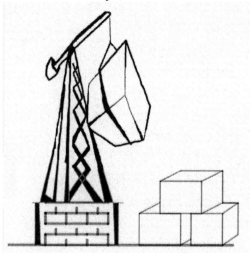

They heard voices shouting and then suddenly felt
themselves being lifted up in the crate

The noise outside grew louder and louder. There was a huge roar of engines and Dippy and Mink were tossed about inside the crate.

"Hold on tight," advised Dippy. "I think we're on our way to Earth!"

With that, they settled down in a corner of the crate, using whatever they could find to make things more comfortable and both were soon fast asleep.

Dippy and Mink must have slept for ages. Dippy awoke first and looked at his computer watch. Many light years had passed but he had no idea where they were or when they would land on Earth. He looked at Mink still sleeping and decided to leave him to rest a while longer, because after all he had been through, he must be very tired.

After what seemed an eternity, Dippy heard the sound of the shuttle's engines change and he felt the spacecraft slow. He nudged Mink.

"Wake up, I think we're landing on Earth."

Mink jumped in excitement and started dancing and singing.

"Quiet," said Dippy, "or someone will hear you. When we land you must stay close by me because I don't know what to expect and we have to get out of here somehow."

The entry through the outer atmosphere of Earth was a bumpy one and the two little aliens had to hold on tight to each other for protection. They landed with a thud amidst a lot of strange noises, presumably from the vast reverse engine boosters. Dippy peered out through a small hole but all he could see was clouds of dust and smoke. Then, as the dust settled, he could see huge steps being pushed towards the shuttle and men, he guessed humans, standing around holding weapons of some kind.

"This isn't going to be easy Mink," said Dippy. "I think our only hope is to stay in the crate and try and escape once we have been lifted off the shuttle."

Mink nodded. "Sounds okay to me."

The pair snuggled back down into a corner. Moments later they heard voices around them and a clanging of chains. Mink hid himself under some old sheets, trying hard to stop his teeth chattering. Then they felt the crate gradually lift into the air, swinging back and forth. Dippy was thrown against the side of the crate and had to put his hand over his mouth to stop himself yelping out in pain. The crate landed with a thump and once again they heard voices as the chains were removed from the crate and then everything was silent.

Dippy put his finger on his lips indicating to Mink to keep quiet. He very carefully stood up and peered over the edge of the crate, sheets still draped over his head and shoulders.

Apart from a human some distance away, the coast was clear and Dippy whispered, "Keep close to me. We'll climb out and hide behind that building over there, the one with the red sign on it."

Mink nodded and, standing on one of the boxes inside the crate, was able to clamber over the side behind Dippy, throwing his bag to the ground as he did so. Once on the ground he scooped up his luggage and ran as fast as he could to the building Dippy had indicated. Once there, both Dippy and Mink sat quietly, pausing to get their breath back.

"Now what?" Mink asked.

"Don't know," replied Dippy. "Let me think for a while."

So there they sat whilst Dippy pondered their next move. At last they were on planet Earth and their adventure could really begin.

Chapter 6

Adventures On Earth

Night began to close in and it became darker. No problem to the little aliens of course. They were used to darkness. They gathered up their belongings and started to walk away from the space station and out onto the big roads. The noise of the traffic and the strange vehicles made Mink hold tight to Dippy's hand.

"I'm tired," moaned Mink. "Can we rest yet?"

"As soon as we find some shelter," replied Dippy. They walked across an open field, delighting in the soft green plants under their feet. They came to a shelter and curled up in one corner, covering themselves with their rugs and both fell fast asleep.

Unbeknown to them, a tramp also sought shelter. He noticed the two little figures huddled in the corner and went over to them. What he saw made him gasp in amazement.

"Now I know I'm going mad," he muttered to himself. "If I didn't know better, I'd say they were aliens like on the telly. They've even got aerials sticking out of their heads. I knew I shouldn't have drunk all that whisky."

He backed away and trundled off to find somewhere else to sleep for the night.

Mink and Dippy awoke next morning, just as it was getting light.

"That's odd," said Dippy, "usually we are asleep when it's light."

They sat quietly for a while, taking in their new surroundings. Roads, cars, people, trees, the blue sky, the green grass, were all new to the little aliens and they were overwhelmed.

"Wow!" said Mink, shaking his head in disbelief.

"Well, we can't stay here all day. For one thing we need to find some food," observed Dippy.

So, gathering up the case and the bag, they set off down the busy street. Although it was early and not too many people were about, they did get some strange looks from passers-by.

"Isn't it amazing," said one lady, "what they can do with make-up and disguises. The little dears must be ready for a party or something. They look just as I imagine creatures from outer space to look like."

Her friend nodded and said, "Amazing, amazing."

Dippy and Mink of course, didn't really understand what people were saying or indeed why they were being stared at but just put it down to humans being friendly.

After walking for quite a time, having looked in numerous shop windows, they saw a burger bar on the other side of the road.

"That looks like a place to get food," said Dippy, "but we have to cross over this road. Hold my hand Mink."

They stood at the edge of the kerb as cars and lorries whizzed past them, wheels rumbling and horns tooting. It was very frightening.

Then two humans approached them and said, "You poor dears. Come on, we will see you safely across the road."

Mink and Dippy looked at each other and shrugged their shoulders. With that, the humans held Mink and Dippy by the hand and took them safely across the road.

"Poor darlings," said the female human. "Fancy letting two little boys out alone in the middle of a city. It really is irresponsible." Then they walked off, muttering.

"That looks like a place to get food", said Dippy, "but we have to cross over this road. Hold my hand Mink".

"Come on," said Dippy, "let's go in here and see if we can get something to eat." They sat at a table near the window so they could watch people walking about. The waitress came over to them and asked what they wanted to eat and drink. The little aliens just looked at her, not understanding.

"Oh I see, dumb are we?" she said crossly. "Well I guess you'll want chicken nuggets and chips and two Cokes like all the other kids. Off to the big fancy dress party are we?"

She didn't get an answer so went off towards the kitchen.

"Two little dumb brats over there," she said to one of the other waitresses. "Kids these days are downright rude."

Meantime Dippy and Mink sat, watching in amazement at all the activity outside. People rushing about carrying little square cases and things like sticks. Cars and lorries were speeding back and forth. It was chaotic.

"Glad I don't live here," said Mink. "It's making my head spin."

Just then the waitress returned and put the food and drink down in front of them. She also placed a piece of paper on the table but as the little aliens couldn't read what was written on it, Dippy screwed it up and threw it on the floor. They poured the liquid into their feeding tubes followed by the food. Mink suddenly spluttered and started to turn blue.

"I think: it's got stuck," he said, massaging his food tube gently. "Ooh, that's better."

"Break it up into little pieces next time," advised Dippy.

Having eaten and drunk the two little aliens got up and walked out of the cafe, completely unaware of the waitress screaming and shouting behind them, "You little devils, come back here. You haven't paid!"

Chapter 7

Orbit The Dog And Party Time!

Dippy and Mink strolled on along the street, revelling in all the attention they were getting.

"You'd think they had never seen an alien before wouldn't you?" said Mink.

Dippy smiled. Mink nudged Dippy and said, "Have you noticed the little creature who has been following us?"

"No," said Dippy turning round. "Oh, isn't he cute?" He stopped and bent down, stroking the creature's soft fur. The dog, for that's what it was, licked Dippy's hand and rubbed his soft furry body against Dippy's legs.

"Let's keep him, please," pleaded Mink. "I've already thought of a name for him."

"Oh yes, and what's that?" asked Dippy, lifting the dog up into his arms.

"Orbit," replied Mink. "I think we should call him Orbit."

"Well, alright. He doesn't seem to belong to anyone around here."

"Yippee!" shouted Mink. "I've always wanted a pet."

"Orbit", replied Mink. "I think we should call him Orbit".

The aliens got tired of walking around. There was so much excitement and so many new experiences. They sat on a park bench and dozed, probably dreaming about everything they had seen. Orbit meanwhile, was having a great time chasing and playing with the other dogs in the park but after a while he returned to Dippy and Mink and, jumping on top of Dippy, gave him a big lick to wake him up. Dippy awoke with a start.

"Get off me you little monster," he laughed.

Mink woke up too with all the commotion and for a while the pair played happily with Orbit, running and chasing about.

Time had raced by and it was starting to get dark.

"Here," said Dippy, "recharge your battery quickly and we will go on a bit further and seek out more food and shelter. I expect Orbit is getting hungry too."

The pair trundled along, past rows and rows of buildings, each with lights showing through the windows. They came to one house where lots of children were milling about inside. Each one was dressed in strange clothes, carrying what looked like a coloured ball on a string.

"I wonder what is going on in there?" said Dippy.

"Let's go and see," replied Mink, skipping ahead, Orbit at his feet.

As they got closer to the house, an adult human came towards them.

"Come on in," she said. "You must be friends of John. Your costumes are marvellous. Your mother must be very good at sewing."

She laughed and gently steered the two little aliens into the house. There were little humans running about everywhere. Laughing, talking, eating and drinking. There was a big table at one end of the room piled high with all manner of different foods and in the centre of the table was a huge round cake with little fires burning on the top. One little human called John, went up to the fires and blew them out. Everyone cheered and started to sing. It was very exciting. Mink wasted no time in popping one thing after another into his food tube until it was full to bursting!

In the centre of the table was a huge round cake.

Then the little human who they called John, opened up lots of boxes of all shapes and sizes and took out from them all manner of strange things. A big male human then came into the room and said something and all the little humans, they were called children, lined up whilst the 'man' walked up and down looking at them. He moved a little girl dressed up with pink wings and a frilly dress to the front of the line. Then he moved a boy, dressed in a black cloak with a tall pointed hat and then he came over to Dippy and Mink and everyone cheered and clapped. A lady came over and gave each of them a box of something. It seemed as though they had won some sort of game. The children then went back to eating and playing but Dippy and Mink, now completely astonished by events, decided it was time to leave and to find somewhere to rest. Outside sat Orbit, waiting patiently.

"Come on little fellow," said Dippy, gathering Orbit up into his arms, "I've got some food for you."

Dippy, Mink and Orbit walked further along the street. People stopped and stared and pointed at them but the aliens took no notice.

"I'm really tired," said Mink.

"You're always tired," replied Dippy, "but I have to admit, it has been a very long day and perhaps we should find somewhere to rest for the night. Look over there at that big building with the tall tower. Let's try to see if we can get in there."

They reached the building, which had a huge, wooden door. Dippy pushed it open and it creaked as he did so. Inside were lots of seats and strange statues, some covered in shiny gold.

"It's a bit scary in here. Are you sure it's safe?" asked Mink, in a trembling voice.

"Well, it is warm and we can curl up in a corner out of sight. Come on," said Dippy.

Orbit snuggled closer into Dippy's chest for warmth and comfort. Before sleeping, Dippy gave Orbit the food he had saved from the party and it wasn't long before all three were fast asleep.

A little while later, actually several space hours had passed, Mink woke up with a start.

He prodded Dippy and said, "Quick! What's that awful noise?"

Dippy sat up and listened, then he laughed out loud.

"It's alright, it's Orbit snoring."

The two little aliens slept peacefully again until they were awoken by the sound of voices.

"Who's that?" whispered Mink.

"Sssh, keep quiet," said Dippy, placing one hand over Mink's mouth and the other around Orbit's muzzle to stop him growling. "Time to move on I think."

The pair got up and crept silently out of the dark building and out into the sunlit street.

Mink rubbed his eye, trying hard to wake up properly, then he shouted, "Hey, we forgot. Let's open those presents we were given at the party. I quite forgot about them."

They sat down on a nearby bench, ripping off the paper to reveal two very smart toy laser guns.

"Wow!" said Dippy. "They're just like the ones the soldiers carry back home. I have always wanted one of my own."

Chapter 8

At The Fair

So it was, two excited little aliens, proudly walked down the street carrying a suitcase, a bag and each with a laser gun hung over his shoulder, Orbit the dog skipping happily at their feet. They came to a park upon which were all manner of very strange things. There was a huge wheel going round with humans sat in little boxes going up and over, screaming and shouting with delight. There were people everywhere. Some were eating strange food like fluffy pink clouds on sticks and cakes with holes in them. There were men calling out, "Roll up, roll up. Win your goldfish here!" Dippy picked Orbit up before he got trodden on.

"Come on you two little boys in fancy dress. Take a ride on the big wheel."

"You know that silver coin you found down the street, Mink? Well, I have been watching and if you give it to that man, I think we can go for a ride on that big wheel."

Mink looked up.

"I am not so sure I want to," he replied.

"Oh come on, don't be a softie. I saw these once in a book about Earth and I've always wanted to try it."

"Yes, I know," said Mink, "but don't you remember Mummy saying what a stupid idea it was?"

Dippy chose to ignore that and pushed Mink forward.

"Give us your money then," said the man.

Mink handed the coin over and he and Dippy clambered into the little compartment and sat down. The man pushed a big bar across the front of them and the wheel started to move slowly, higher and higher into the air they went. You could see for miles.

"I feel very sick," he said. Indeed he had turned a funny colour.

At the very top, the wheel ground to a stop with lots of creaking noises. Mink grabbed Dippy's arm.

"I feel very sick," he said.

Indeed he had turned a funny colour. Not green like sick human beings but a kind of blue.

"You don't look too good," said Dippy.

Mink closed his eye and moaned, "Get me down, get me down!"

To his relief, the wheel started to move slowly until their little cab reached the ground again. The man moved towards them and undid the big, metal bar.

"Oh my, you look awful, lad. You had better go and sit down and don't go eating anything for a while!"

He went off chuckling to himself.

"I'm glad he finds it funny," said Mink.

A lady came over to them and offered Mink some clear liquid in a cup.

"Drink this my love, you'll soon feel better."

Mink took the cup and poured the cool liquid into his food tube. The lady looked on in amazement and lost for words, took the cup from Mink and walked away with a very strange look on her face.

Mink and Dippy spent quite a while at the fair. It was all very exciting.

"I'm getting hungry," whimpered Mink.

"Me too," said Dippy. "I think we must leave here and go and look for some food."

The pair reluctantly left the noise and the excitement of the fair and walked back along the road towards a shop they had passed earlier.

"In here," said Dippy, grabbing Mink's hand and pulling him into the shop.

They wandered around looking at all the peculiar foods.

"Hey Dippy, look. It's like a little tree." Mink held up a sprig of broccoli. "And look, orange fingers!" He pointed to some carrots.

Because Mink insisted on examining just about everything, it took ages to get round the shop but they had selected some biscuits and some chocolate and two cartons of orange juice. They took everything to the lady at the checkout.

"That will be four pounds and twenty pence please," she said.

The two little aliens looked at one another in disbelief. They had no money at all.

Then a kindly lady in the queue behind them, said to the shop assistant, "Oh don't make a fuss. I will pay for everything. The darlings look so sweet in their costumes."

Dippy and Mink smiled at the lady, gathered up their goodies and left the shop.

"Wow! That was lucky," said Dippy. "I didn't realise you have to pay for food."

Chapter 9

Time To Go Home

Back outside, the boys found themselves a seat to sit on and enjoyed their food and drink.

"Tell you what," said Dippy, "today is the day we have to start our journey back to the space station in order to get the shuttle back home."

"Oh no," sighed Mink, "I like it here, though I must admit, it will be nice to get home. I have missed Mummy."

"Well, now we know how it's done, maybe we could come back again one day," said Dippy comfortingly, "that is, if the parents don't ground us forever!"

Using their direction finder and the computer, the boys found their way back to the space station and onto the shuttle bound for Dyfuss.

Huddled up in a corner of a crate, the two aliens talked about their first adventure on Earth until they were tired of talking and they fell fast asleep.

Much, much later, they awoke as they once again felt themselves being lifted high up into the air, suspended by a chain from a huge crane. As before, they waited until they felt the bump as they were lowered back onto the ground. When it was safe to do so, they clambered out of the crate and took refuge inside one of the many outbuildings surrounding the space station. Dippy spent quite a time plotting their journey home. Across the desert, through the towns of Bathos and Metronia, round the Frozen Forest to Acad and from there to Dyfuss and home.

Their journey took many light years until at last they found themselves outside their home once again.

"Gosh, I am glad to be back," said Mink.

"Quiet!" said Dippy crossly. "We've still got to get inside without being caught!"

He clutched Mink's hand and took him round the back of the building.

"Put your things on the ground, climb on my shoulders and reach up to open my bedroom window," instructed Dippy.

"OK, no problem," said Mink who had grown up a great deal during their Earth adventure.

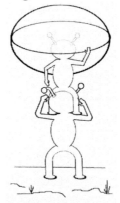

"Put your things on the ground, climb on my shoulders and reach up to open my bedroom window."

Once inside, Mink called down to Dippy, "Throw up everything, one item at a time."

So up went the bag, the suitcase, the rug and several other things like their new laser guns.

"Wait there," whispered Dippy to Orbit. "I'll let *you* in later."

Then Mink lowered down a piece of rope on to which Dippy held tight as Mink hauled him up an inch at a time.

Now totally exhausted, both Dippy and Mink crawled into their beds and fell fast asleep but not before thinking of the trouble they would be in next morning.

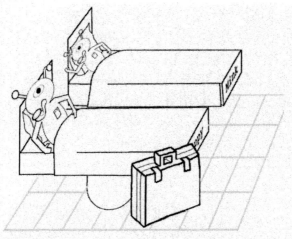

"You are such a sleepy-head" you would think you had been round the world and back!"

"Come on, come on," said Dippy's Mum, shaking him. "It's time to get up. You are such a sleepy-head you would think you had been round the world and back!" she laughed. "Oh and I found this little creature crying outside. We will look after it until I find out who owns it."

With that she lifted Orbit onto the bed. She left the room, still chuckling to herself. Dippy sat up, puzzled that his mum hadn't got really mad with him. He looked at his calendar to see what day it was then, smiling, he went over to Mink's bed, Orbit following closely behind.

"Is Mummy really angry?" asked Mink, wiping his eye.

"No," said Dippy, "and do you know why? I had forgotten that it is the sleep season, when time on Dyfuss stands still for almost fifty light years, so they haven't even realised we have been away!"

"That's fantastic!" said Mink. "Come on, let's get up and go and tell our friends about our adventures. They will never believe us!"

"They certainly won't!" agreed Dippy.

THE END